The Story of Our Holidays

DIWALI

Joanna Ponto and Michelle Parker-Rock

Enslow Publishing
101 W. 23rd Street
Suite 240
New York, NY 10011
USA
enslow.com

Published in 2017 by Enslow Publishing, LLC.
101 W. 23rd Street, Suite 240, New York, NY 10011

Library of Congress Cataloging-in-Publication Data
Names: Ponto, Joanna, author. | Parker-Rock, Michelle, author.
Title: Diwali / Joanna Ponto and Michelle Parker-Rock.
Description: New York, NY : Enslow Pub., [2017] | Series: The story of our holidays | Includes bibliographical references and index. | Audience: Grades 4-6.
Identifiers: LCCN 2016001032| ISBN 9780766076488 (library bound) | ISBN 9780766076464 (pbk.) | ISBN 9780766076471 (6-pack)
Subjects: LCSH: Diwali--Juvenile literature. | Fasts and feasts--Hinduism.
Classification: LCC BL1239.82.D58 P37 2016 | DDC 294.5/36--dc23
LC record available at http://lccn.loc.gov/2016001032

Printed in the United States of America

To Our Readers: We have done our best to make sure all websites in this book were active and appropriate when we went to press. However, the author and the publisher have no control over and assume no liability for the material available on those websites or on any websites they may link to. Any comments or suggestions can be sent by e-mail to customerservice@enslow.com.

Portions of this book originally appeared in the book *Diwali: The Hindu Festival of Lights, Feasts, and Family* by Michelle Parker-Rock.

Photo Credits: Cover, p. 1 Kaustav Bhattacharya/Moment/Getty Images; p. 4 imagedb.com/Shutterstock.com; p. 8 Indian School/Ashmolean Museum/Bridgeman Images; p. 11 National Museum of India/Bridgeman Images; pp. 13, 26 © AP Images; p. 16 ImagesBazaar/Getty Images; p. 17 Hemant Mehta/Thinkstock; p. 20 iStock.com/szefei; p. 21 Pikoso.kz/Shutterstock.com; p. 22 vm2002/iStock/Thinkstock; p. 23 Vectoraart/iStock/Thinkstock; p. 25 giddavr1952/ iStock/Thinkstock; p. 27 uniquely india/Getty Images; p. 29 Cheryl Bavaro.

Contents

The Hindu holiday Diwali is a celebration of good over evil. It is the festival of lights.

Chapter 1

The Ramayana

On the holiday of Diwali, people celebrate with strings of lights, candles, and firecrackers. Diwali is the Hindu festival of lights. It is a celebration of light over dark and of good over evil. Hindus celebrate this holiday by telling the tale of the prince Rama. His exciting story follows.

Rama and Sita

A long time ago in India, Rama was born. Rama was the oldest son of King. He had dark skin, dark eyes, and black curly hair. Rama was an avatar of the Hindu god Vishnu. That means he was a god in human form. Vishnu had given Rama his spirit because Rama had a special purpose on Earth.

Rama was strong, handsome, and loved by all. He was always successful. Everyone knew that he would someday become king.

In a nearby kingdom, the good King Janaka wanted his beautiful daughter, Sita, to marry the bravest and strongest prince in all of India. Sita was born with the spirit of Vishnu's wife, the goddess Lakshmi. She was graceful with long, flowing hair. She, too, was loved by everyone.

"My daughter will marry the prince who can string my bow," said Sita's father. Many princes tried, but only Rama could string the bow. Rama and Sita had a grand wedding and lived happily for many years.

"Rama will be the next king," Rama's father said. But Rama's stepmother wanted her son, Bharat, to be king. She asked the king to send Rama away. The king had once promised his wife that he would grant her two wishes, so he told Rama to leave the kingdom.

Exiled

Rama, Sita, and Rama's brother, Lakshman, went to live in the forest. The forest was filled with many wild beasts and evil spirits. Rama and Lakshman fought many of them and always won.

Before long, they were visited by an evil woman. She was the sister of Ravan, the monster king with ten heads from the city of Lanka. When Ravan's sister saw Rama, she fell in love with him and asked him to marry her.

"I cannot marry you," he said. "I love Sita. She is my wife." The monster king's sister did not like Rama's answer. So she tried to harm Sita. Luckily, Sita was saved by Lakshman.

Hurt and angry, Ravan's sister left the forest. But she soon returned with the evil Ravan. When Ravan saw Sita, he fell in love with her. He wanted her to be his wife. Sita said no. So Ravan tricked her and took her to his castle in Lanka.

Along the way, Sita threw her scarf and a sparkling jewel to the magical monkeys in the forest. She hoped the monkeys would help Rama find her.

Rebirth

The three main Hindu gods are Brahma, the creator of the universe; Vishnu, the protector of the universe; and Shiva, the destroyer of the world. According to Hindu belief, Vishnu was born as a human many times. Each time he was born, a new story was created. When Vishnu was born as Rama, his wife, Lakshmi, was born as Sita.

The Hunt for Sita

Rama and Lakshman wandered through the enchanted forest looking for Sita. Along the way, Rama met a creature that was under a magic

Rama and Lakshman shoot at Ravan, the monster king with ten heads, in the Ramayana.

spell. Rama freed it, and in return the creature helped Rama. It sent Rama to see the monkey king. "The monkey king will help you save Sita," it said.

The monkey king showed Rama what Sita had dropped from Ravan's flying chariot. "This is Sita's scarf and jewel," said the monkey king. "Now go see the god of the wind. He will help you next."

Rama found the god of the wind and gave him his ring. "Show this to Sita when you see her. Then she will know that you have found her for me," said Rama.

On the way, the god of the wind met a vulture with burnt wings. The sun god had promised the vulture that his wings would grow strong again if he helped Rama. So the vulture told the god of the wind that he heard a woman in a chariot calling to Rama as she flew by. "The chariot belongs to King Ravan of Lanka," he said. The god of the wind thanked the vulture and took off again to find Sita.

The god of the wind found Sita in Lanka. "Tell Rama that I will not live much longer without him," she cried.

The god of the wind returned to Rama. "Now I will show you how to get to the kingdom of Lanka," the god of the wind told him.

A Path of Light

With new hope, Rama crossed the miles of ocean between India and Lanka. When he arrived, he told Ravan, "Give me my wife or I will destroy you." But the fearless Ravan decided to fight Rama.

Ravan flew out of his castle and shot an arrow at Rama. Rama asked the gods for help. The arrow turned and struck Ravan's heart.

When Rama and Sita were together again, Rama's father appeared. He told Rama that everything had gone as planned. "This is what the gods wanted you to do," he said. "You have destroyed the evil King Ravan. Now you and Sita can return to our kingdom as king and queen."

There was a grand celebration for King Rama and Queen Sita. The royal families ordered that the cities and kingdoms be lit with rows of glittering lamps to welcome them home. Rama and Sita lived joyfully for a long time.

The Festival of Lights

This tale about Rama is called the Ramayana. The holiday of Diwali celebrates the story of Rama and Sita.

During the festival of Diwali, thousands of little oil lamps are lit just as they were for Rama and Sita's return. The lights are also meant to welcome the goddess Lakshmi, who is said to bring gifts of wealth, good fortune, and success. That is why Diwali is also called the festival of lights. We will talk about more ways that Diwali is celebrated in the next few chapters.

Rama and his brothers all get married in this celebratory scene from the Ramayana.

Chapter 2

An Ancient Holiday

No one is exactly sure when Diwali was first celebrated. This is because it began in ancient India before history was written down.

Thanks for the Harvest

At that time, many people were farmers and merchants. Merchants bought and sold what the farmers grew. The people were thankful when the monsoons, a time of heavy rain, ended.

The people were also thankful for the crops they harvested for the New Year. A harvest is a gathering of food that is grown on farms and in gardens. The people thanked the gods for giving them a good crop.

Some stories say that the god Vishnu gave the people the festival of Diwali to celebrate their harvest. Today, there are farm areas in northern India where people still think of Diwali as a harvest festival.

Other Ideas

There are other ideas about the first Diwali, too. Some people think it may have been to celebrate the marriage of the god Vishnu and the goddess Lakshmi. Others think that the holiday began like the story in Chapter 1 when Rama returns to become king. But whichever story is believed to be true, all Hindus agree that Diwali is a holiday to be enjoyed.

Diwali may have started as a festival to celebrate the harvest.

Chapter 3

The Hindu Religion

Indian Americans and Hindu people all around the globe celebrate Diwali. Hinduism is one of the oldest and largest religions in the world. People are not certain how Hinduism started, but we know that it began in the country of India more than four thousand years ago.

Hindu Spirits

Many Hindus believe in a spirit called Brahman that is in all things all the time. A spirit is an energy that does not have any shape or form. This means that Brahman is in all people, animals, and plants.

Hindus also believe that everybody has a soul or a spirit called Atman. Hinduism teaches that when a person dies, the person's soul can be born again as another person or other living thing. This is called reincarnation. How a person is reborn in the next life depends on how they live in their present life. You can be born to a better life if you do more good actions than bad actions. These actions are called karma.

The Vedas

Sanskrit is a language that was used in India a long time ago. The oldest and most blessed Hindu books are written in Sanskrit. The most important of these are the Vedas. The Vedas are holy books for Hindus like the Bible is for Christians or the Torah is for Jews. The Vedas teach people how to live their lives as Hindus.

Hinduism is a part of everyday Hindu life. People in different parts of India and around the world practice Hinduism in many ways. Hindus can choose to study, pray, treat others kindly, or meditate to live a life of good karma.

Hindus and Diwali

Diwali is one of the main Hindu festivals. This means that it is a big religious holiday for Indian Americans and Hindu people in India and other countries. Hindus show their respect for this day in temples, at street shrines, and at shrines in their homes. A shrine is a place where people pray.

Diwali is a religious holiday. Families pray to shrines to show respect.

One main theme of Diwali is light. People celebrate by lighting candles, lamps, and fireworks.

The name Diwali comes from the Sanskrit word *dipavali*. *Dipavali* means "row of lights." That is why Diwali is also called the festival of lights. On Diwali, oil lamps, candles, and colored electric lights shine brightly in Hindu homes, businesses, and temples.

Indian families welcome Diwali in lots of ways. They share many interesting stories about gods and goddesses. These stories help us understand more about Diwali.

Chapter 4

Preparations

Indians use a lunar calendar. This is different from the calendar used in the United States. A lunar month is the time between one new moon and the next new moon. Each lunar month lasts twenty-nine-and-a-half days.

Diwali arrives in the lunar month of Kartika. It begins just before the night of the new moon. In America, Diwali occurs at the end of October or the beginning of November.

Clean House, New Clothes

Hundreds of thousands of families in the United States, Canada, and other countries have lots to do to get ready to celebrate Diwali. They usually begin by making their homes very clean. They believe that the goddess Lakshmi only brings wealth and good fortune to very clean homes.

Many families buy new clothes for Diwali. Some people choose to wear Indian-style clothes. Women and girls may choose to wear saris. These are dresses made from colorful cloth that is wrapped around the body. They may also wear long, fancy shirts over baggy pants. Men and boys may wear loose-fitting shirts called kurtas over baggy cotton pants. Other people wear American-style dresses, shirts, and pants.

People do not only shop for new clothes on Diwali. They also like to buy and wear new gold jewelry. Before they wear the new jewelry on Diwali, they perform a puja and offer it as a gift to the goddess Lakshmi.

Hindu Shrines

A puja is a Hindu prayer service that is held in a temple or shrine. Hindu shrines can be almost anywhere. They can be in homes, schools, shops, or even in the street. In a shrine, there is usually a picture or statue of the god or goddess to be worshiped. During the puja food, flowers, sweets, and holy water are offered to the god or goddess.

Hindus and Indian Americans wear new, colorful clothing and gold jewelry on Diwali.

Food is an important part of the Diwali holiday. People celebrate with delectable special foods and sweet treats.

Diwali Treats

People love to eat sweet treats and delicious foods during Diwali. Barfi is a fudge treat that is made with milk, sugar, nuts, fruits, flour, and sometimes even vegetables! Rasgullas are milk dumplings dipped in sugar syrup. Jalebis is another favorite treat. A jalebis looks like a twisted pretzel. It is made from a flour batter that is fried in butter and then soaked in a sugar syrup. Lassi is a drink made with yogurt, fruit, and spices. You can make mango lassi using the recipe on the next page.

Mango Lassi*

Ingredients:

2 ripe mangos
1½ cups (350 mL) plain yogurt, unsweetened
2 tablespoons (30 mL) honey
½ teaspoon (2.5 mL) cardamom powder
2 cups (280 g) ice

Directions:

1. Peel the mangos, remove the stone with a large spoon, and cut the mango fruit into bite-sized pieces.
2. Put the mango pieces into a blender or food processor and blend them until they are almost liquid. This is called a puree.
3. Add the yogurt, honey, cardamom, and ice to the mangos, and keep blending until the liquid is frothy.
4. Pour into a glass with more ice.

For a frozen version:

1. Pour the frothy liquid into Popsicle trays or small plastic cups.
2. Place a Popsicle stick into the middle of each cup.
3. Freeze for at least 6 hours.

* Adult supervision required.

During Diwali, families enjoy going out to eat. Restaurants prepare many different kinds of curried foods. Curry is a mixture of spices that is used to flavor chicken, vegetables, eggs, and other popular Indian dishes. These foods are eaten with rice and flat wheat breads called chapattis. Pakooras are vegetables that have been coated in chickpea flour and deep-fried in oil until they are golden brown. Potato samosas are little pastries filled with potatoes that are also deep-fried.

Many Indian people like to send each other Diwali greeting cards. The cards may have pictures of the goddess Lakshmi or the god Ganesh, who is usually shown with the head of an elephant. Hindu people pray to Ganesh before starting something new. The cards wish good fortune and good luck in the New Year.

There are many things to do to celebrate this wonderful holiday. Colorful lights and tiny oil lamps are lit. Diwali is here. Now, it is time to celebrate!

Chapter 5

The Festival of Lights

People all around the world celebrate Diwali. In India, the holiday may last for four or five days. In the United States and Canada, it is usually only celebrated for one day. Diwali is a time for everyone to be happy. It is a time to be hopeful about the coming year.

Diwali Customs

During Diwali, businesspeople close their accounts. They pay money that they owe. Then they say a prayer called a Chopda Puja to bring good luck to their businesses. Shopkeepers may offer lower prices in their stores. Customers often purchase something made of gold or silver or buy a new kitchen tool for good luck.

Many doorways to homes, shops, temples, and restaurants are decorated with colorful designs called *rangoli*. Rangoli is a very old art form that uses colored flour to form patterns, pictures, and words on the ground. Today, powdered white stone may be used, as well. Pictures of flowers, animals, gods, goddesses, temples, and diye (oil lamps) are common rangoli designs. Sometimes, even small footprints are drawn to welcome Lakshmi.

Everyone dresses in new or newly washed clothes. Some women and girls decorate their skin with henna. Henna is a plant. The henna leaves are dried and ground into a powder, which is mixed with water to make a paste. The paste can be used to paint designs on the skin. The designs can be simple or fancy.

Doorways and entrances are decorated with colorful designs called rangoli.

How People Celebrate

Lakshmi Puja is performed on the night of Diwali. Prayers are said, lamps are lit, and songs are sung. Sweet

Diwali Lights

A *diya* is a traditional oil lamp made from baked clay. Before people had electric lights, they used diye (the plural of diya) on Diwali. The first diya would be lit, and it would be used to light all the other diye in the house. Some people still use diye, but candles, electric lights, or handmade lanterns are more common today.

treats, small puffs of rice called khil, fruit, and flowers are offered to Lakshmi. Then to show respect, the children touch their elders' feet. Diwali pujas are held at Hindu temples and at home.

Families and friends often get together during Diwali. They may attend public events where stories of the Hindu gods are told with Indian music and dancing. People visit each other at home, too. Card games are common among the adults. Activities such as Light the Flame on the Diya

People decorate their homes with colorful garlands and glowing lights during Diwali.

(see page 28) are fun for children. In recent years, giving gifts has become popular, as well.

When the night of Diwali arrives, diye, candles, and electric lights are lit. The lights shine from doorways, windows, rooftops, courtyards, and gardens. The lights flicker along streets and in markets. The night glitters with the glow of all the lights of Diwali.

When it is time for the Diwali meal, plates of food are shared. Sweet treats are enjoyed by all. Circles of sugar called patashe are a favorite candy to enjoy after dinner.

In some cities and towns, fireworks are allowed. The sky becomes bright with colorful patterns. People set off small firecrackers and light sparklers. It is believed that the loud noises of the firecrackers keep evil away.

Diwali, the Hindu festival of lights, may be the best-known Indian holiday. It is loved by all who celebrate it. Diwali brings joy and happiness to Hindus and Indian people each New Year.

Children enjoy the glittering lights and fireworks of Diwali.

Diwali Craft*

You can make a fun game for your friends and family to play on Diwali!

Here are the supplies you will need:

orange or yellow felt
brown felt
black or white felt
cardboard
black marker
safety scissors
white glue
yarn or string
a scarf
glitter glue (optional)
adhesive Velcro

Directions:

1. Draw the shape of a diya on the brown felt. Carefully cut it out.
2. Cut a piece of black or white felt so it is the same size as your piece of cardboard. Glue the felt to the cardboard. Let it dry.
3. Glue the diya onto the middle of the black or white felt. Let it dry.
4. With the marker, draw flame shapes on the orange or yellow felt. Cut out one flame for each player. Add adhesive Velcro on the back of the flames. If you like, add glitter glue to make your flame sparkle!
5. Glue the ends of a piece of yarn to the back of the cardboard. After the glue has dried, hang the cardboard on the wall with the felt side facing out.

Light the Flame on the Diya

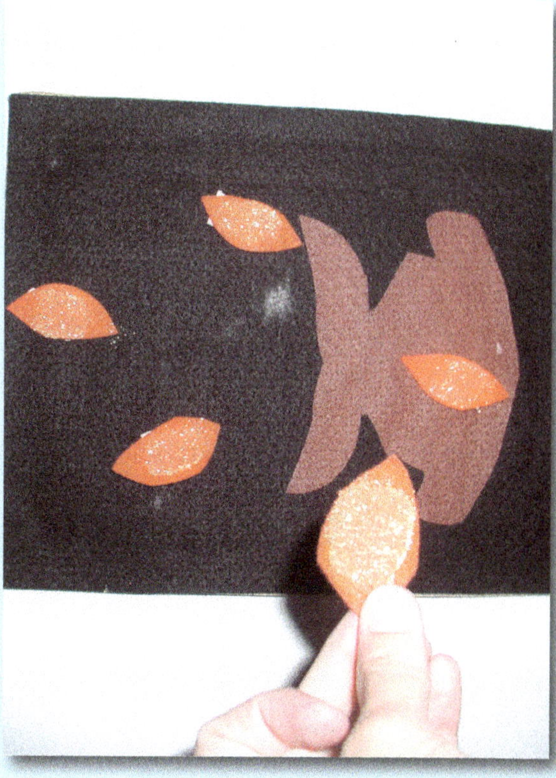

How to play:

1. Give each player a flame.
2. Blindfold each player for his or her turn.
3. Turn the player three times as you say this rhyme:

   Diwali is the day,
   When diye light the way.
   So play this little game,
   And try to light the
   flame.

4. Each player tries to put his or her flame at the end of the wick. The winner is the person whose flame is closest!

*Safety note: Be sure to ask for help from an adult, if needed, to complete this project.

Glossary

diya—A clay oil lamp.

exile—Being driven out of one's country.

Hinduism—A religion that began in India more than four thousand years ago.

karma—An action that affects the form of a new life when a person is reborn.

puja—A ceremony in which offerings are made to a god or goddess.

reincarnation—The belief that the soul of a person can be born again.

ritual—A religious ceremony.

Sanskrit—The ancient language of India.

shrine—A holy place to pray and worship.

temple—A building meant for worship and prayer.

Vedas—Ancient Hindu religious books.

Learn More

Books

Howard, Pippa, and Jan Moffitt. *A Story of Diwali: The Festival of Light.* Rickmansworth, England: PJ Books, 2012.

Murray, Julie. *Diwali.* Edina, MN: ABDO Publishing Company, 2014.

Pettiford, Rebecca. *Diwali.* Minneapolis, MN: Bullfrog Books, 2015.

Sood, Sana Hoda, and Rubina Hoda. *Diwali: A Cultural Adventure.* Herndon, VA: Mascot Books, 2013.

Websites

AHC Arts and Crafts

artistshelpingchildren.org/diwaliartscraftsideasprojectskids.html

This site has instructions for a wide variety of Diwali crafts for kids of all ages!

Activity Village

www.activityvillage.co.uk/diwali

Check out fun Diwali crafts, coloring pages, puzzles, and more.

KidsGen Diwali Page

kidsgen.com/events/diwali/diwali_quiz.htm

This page has a great quiz that you and your friends can take to test your knowledge about Diwali.

Index